POP HITS

Partituras para aficionados al piano

MA
NON
TROPPO

©2021, Miguel Ángel Fernández Pérez

©2021, Redbook Ediciones, s. l., Barcelona

Diseño de cubierta: Regina Richling

ISBN: 978-84-18703-15-7

Depósito legal: B-16.178-2021

Impreso por Ingrabar, Industrias Gráficas Barcelona, c/ Perú. 144, 08020 Barcelona

Impreso en España - *Printed in Spain*

POP HITS

Partituras para aficionados al piano

POP HITS

Partituras para aficionados al piano

Memories
Maroon 5

- 6 -

Thinking Out Loud

Ed Sheeran

The Scientist
Coldplay

We Found Love

Rihanna

Skin

Rag'n'Bone Man

On Top of the World

Imagine Dragons

Warrior

Demi Lovato

rit ...

A Thousand Years

Christina Perry

Secrets

OneRepublic

Beautiful

Christina Aguilera

Epiphany
BTS

- 32 -

Just the Way You Are

Bruno Mars

Just You and I

Tom Walker

The Winner Takes It All

ABBA

- 42 -

Someone You Loved

Lewis Capaldi

What About Us

Pink

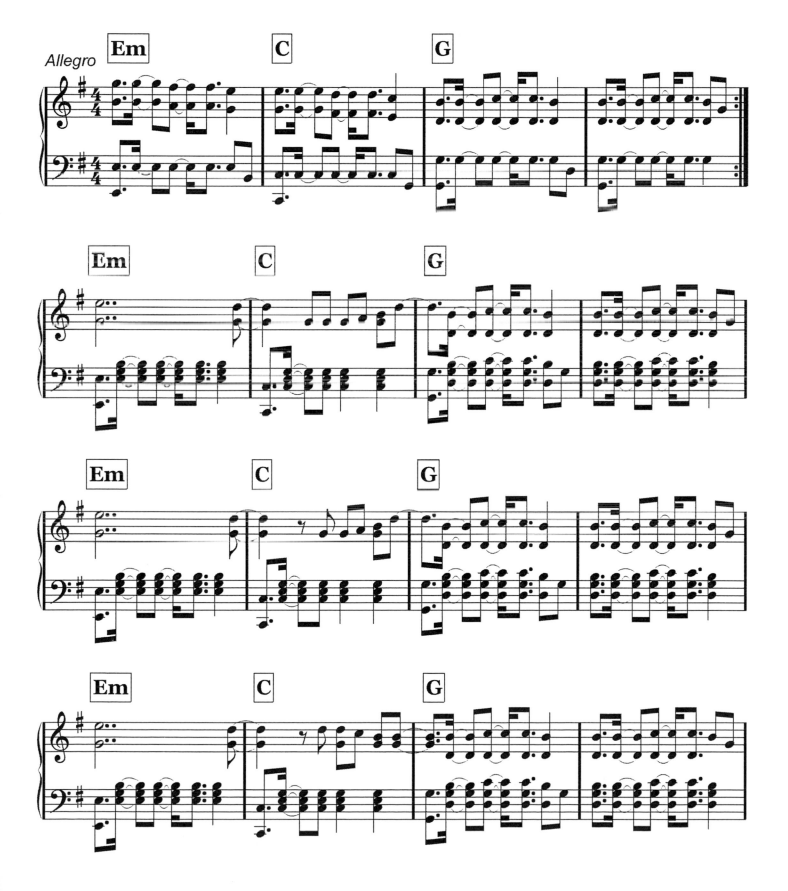

Somewhere Only We Know

Keane

You´re Beautiful

James Blunt

Spider´s Web

Katie Melua

We Are the World

Michael Jackson & Lionel Richie

Perfect

Ed Sheeran

Demons

Imagine Dragons

Wake Me Up
When September Ends

Green Day

My Immortal

Evanescence

Someone Like You
Adele

- 78 -

She´s the One

Robbie Williams

Impossible

James Arthur

Girls Like You
Maroon 5

Say Something

A Great Big World

Heal the World

Michael Jackson

- 94 -

Angels

Robbie Williams

Before You Go
Lewis Capaldi

Empire State of Mind

Alicia Keys

Love Is in the Picture

Jamie Cullum

Runaway

The Corrs

Just Give Me a Reason

Pink

Chiquitita

ABBA

Euphoria

Loreen

Apologize
OneRepublic

Viva la vida

Coldplay

Partituras para aficionados al piano

MA
NON
TROPPO

musicainvisible

Redbook
ediciones